MW01601212

deep kiss

POEMS BY

SHERRY KEARNS

DOS MADRES

2013

DOS MADRES PRESS INC.

P.O.Box 294, Loveland, Ohio 45140
www.dosmadres.com   editor@dosmadres.com

Dos Madres is dedicated to the belief that the small press is essential
to the vitality of contemporary literature as a carrier of the new voice,
as well as the older, sometimes forgotten voices of the past. And in an
ever more virtual world, to the creation of fine books pleasing to the
eye and hand.

Dos Madres is named in honor of Vera Murphy and Libbie Hughes,
the "Dos Madres" whose contributions have made this press possible.

Dos Madres Press, Inc. is an Ohio Not For Profit Corporation and a
501 (c) (3) qualified public charity. Contributions are tax deductible.

Executive Editor: Robert J. Murphy

Illustration & Book Design: Elizabeth H. Murphy
www.illusionstudios.net

Typset in Adobe Garamond Pro & Killigraphy
Cover image is a detail from the painting The Kiss
by Francesco Hayez, 1859

ISBN 978-1-939929-02-0
Library of Congress Control Number: 2013940949

First Edition

For Roger

TABLE OF CONTENTS

masters and muses

imperfectives

love in the second half of life

deep kiss

Deep Kiss

Life,
whoremaster,
put your tongue
in my mouth
so what I tell
has no limits
but the strength
of your desire
for whatever
you can do.

The Blue Vase

Next to the window there is a vase
In the sun--pale as nude
So one could almost trace
The veins of a woman
Curved in blue.

I will send it to you.
Perhaps when you see
It clung to light
You will remember me.

One Good Fuck

Discard the negative
associations here--
think what Lawrence
meant when using this
our plain English
that is the mud of springtime,
good and dark and wet,
from which new grows up--
its short vowel's a little grunt
over the work we must do for it.

Think this way about it--
(just once as friends
because it was a
glorious spring day)
how it resembles
a wine glass that
was a gift both too expensive
and irresistible which
came of true generosity,
that overflow of spirit
which knows even if
the glass gets broken--
as glass does with use--
there'd remain not just
memory of a lovely vessel
but of the giving and
the taking of it.

Satisfactory

I am awake
in the wall
of satisfaction,
aware

how air
blows up
my back

empty with possibility.

In A Snowstorm

As maple trees, which partly disappear
when storm settles upon them, their
twigs blending into the grey air
until only branches and trunks are seen,
you are, when troubled, blunted and severe,
delicacy invisible, though I know it there;
it is by this absence I am made aware
of my expectations for what's unseen
to return, constant, in the changed air.

The Athletic Heart

The beat of the athletic heart is slow.
Its measure made by distance, it goes on
when the mind rebels over repeated miles.
The runner's heart is a metronome,
training the mind: go on go on.
Any heart is athletic for love, rushes blood.
When the mind slips from it,
the heart stays, calls the mind back:
come on come on come on.
Over long distance, words fade;
by its measured sounding the athletic heart
brings round the mind it trained.

Remembering Gerry DiGuisto

I hope Death
came to you
with her soft, generous mouth
and kissed you good,
then pressed her body
warm against yours,
rubbed up a little and said
Come on, honey

and that's why
you're so suddenly gone.

From The Sand

Some thing terrible
must have
its place

no need to name

takes place;

while
at the time
places fill

a voice from the sand
says
sand.

March & April

I

In the snow
The children have
Written TRUE LOVE.

I pass it twice
For fun,
Smile
Up at you.

When it snowed full
Not even a shadow was left.

II

Talk to myself I
Can't tell how
I sound, what
My voice
Makes.

What Shall We Do

What shall we do after the house is built?
It has taken two years to fit
Each board carefully, to nail
Them all in place, to secure us
Against wind.

Could we leave it if we chose,
Once we have made it to hold strong,
Planted--you, trees and I, flowers--
And slept in it?

I could stand by one of the windows
To see you plant, and you,
If you would look, could see me
Watching you move among the winds
We won't let in.

I would live in this house
And pick the flowers and
Taste the fruit the trees bear.

The Search

Someone is searching
among deep pink tongues

one of many
looking and
looking

for a source
of green shadows

and the loose
lush

they intercept
here-
upon.

Bleeding Heart

Of the succession of pink and white hearts,
there is a gradual decline in size
until at stem's end the smallest
punctuates, as if a statement of tender thought,
their conclusion.
In their constancy, spring after spring,
they extend from center, reach over the foliage
to whisper their blossoms in gentle sentences,
phrasing each shape
until the final syllable repeats and silences
what we have been glad to hear.

The Scent Of Yellow Freesias

The scent of freesias today put me in a room
among old friends and set me before a window,
vase in hand; though the wet street promised spring,
the odor of the flowers had changed season in me.
I was green, at winter's window paused
before going out in sunlight to meet my lover;
after, I would come home to friends, this fragrant room.
That was a spring long ago.
Now I plant freesia bulbs to force for that season,
tend the flats and wait, impatient for their blooming.
It's not that I'm unable to recall
when I was young and the seasons were inside me,
but those friends are scattered, my old lover gone,
I live in a different place.
It is the scent of freesias that remains unchanged.
When I bend to them, hose forgotten in my hand,
spring shapes a golden bell,
within the thin tissue of its walls, a room,
and I, the attar of that perfumed air.

The Maple In Blossom

So many bees came to the maple tree,
their humming was audible in the house.
The tree, shimmering with their movement,
appeared iridescent. We, too, show in this way,
how full of moving blood we are in flower.

Language

Language fleshes the skin over our bones,
its lips murmur names to us, fingers
explore every place and thing, calling
them properly, singing to us;
silent when there is nothing to say.

The Equestrienne

We should speak of what we love.
Though duty, which I love, too,
often keeps me from it,
I would, as soon as anything,
be astride in ring or woods.
My years spent learning to stay
with a horse now afford me this:
I can stay without thought,
empty-mindedly respond
in measure to his response to me.
Like a mother rocking an infant,
my legs hold my mount
as he moves under me.
Here's a moment's perfection:
his stride's offspring of skill.
Seat's balance, still hands and legs,
vary with the horse, aren't mine,
are made by his mouth and gaits out of me.
It is the movement, invisible in it,
that I love; each stride complete
feels as endless as we think love and we should be.

In Training

Here's why
a woman loves dressage:
her horse submits to her
as she submits her body
to her husband,

as he submits his
to the tack and aides
of life--
          oh yes, lightness
and harmony--but

first there is rhythm, those daily circles
and going forward, always forward,
straight ahead and strong, in self-carriage
yet always submitting, always in work,

until there is
but one will
guiding the ride

and then there can be art.

Answer To Dr. Rhodes

Did Yeats go to bed with Maude Gonne?
It doesn't matter,
he wanted to.
Barstools and beds
are made hot
with things undone:
poems written,
whole lives or part
lived under a shadow
or in the light
of a single act's possibility.
I am not sorry for that.

Pantheon

What I write
about my true love
is also true
of you and yours.

He must be Eros
when no other god
will do, and though
never the great Jehovah,

he has proved
salvation
upon me.
You,

being you,
will know
what I mean.

DNA

Double helix's running stitch
bastes us crazy quilts together,
desire embroiders; every seam
under the point of the needle.

Seventeen

— continuing a conversation with Jack Gilbert

"Do you repine...
do you wish...
do you think of when
you were seventeen
and in the miracle
of your beauty?"
the old poet asked me
though his face beautiful still.

I should have said,
"No, because the world
is seventeen and always
will be seventeen
in the trees' bearing,
in luminous snowfall,
seventeen in clay and loam
fresh tilled or fallow,
seventeen, the pure sand."

That's what I should
have said, not just
"No, and anyway
we can't go back;
youth is our spent coin
but look what we've
bought with it."

I should have said,
"The young stars are laughing
in the ever-young sky
because soon we're going
to be with them."

After Reading *News of the Universe*

Robert Bly is taking care of me--
he and lesser names
though not lesser men--
and what they do is search
through the universal pandemic
for poetry that is immune
to our deadly diseases of
ego and will, even this common cold,
and transfuse that blood into me
or any who need it to be well.
It's the poems that take care
of us all and poetry
chooses who will survive
affliction and contagion,
keeping its life alive.

Philip Roth In A Dream

In my dream of Philip Roth
the novelist appeared as a bum,
dirty, slovenly, and common,
contrary to the man gracefully
wearing dust jackets in my library.
This must be who he would be
if he could assume--looking
into my private life and seeing
there for his fictionalizing
the base and banal
the reductive and real
composite behind and below
my literate life whose taste
chooses Roth's writing--
the character my character is wed to
in dream's domestic drama
of American life, that which
compels an author to tell it
because it is his own
if it is ours.

masters and muses

Life Under Water

— for Bill Bronk

My 2nd favorite poet's is a secret life.
He cooks without recipe, writes of another world,
lives alone. In public, he talks of common things,
seeming to be with us. He is as far
as the ocean floor, miles deep, tracked by clams
that in sightless movement eat their way
below waters clean or foul.
They take and turn the sediment.
He lives underwater, writes of it.
The poems trace through him their own blind life,
mark as they go the veins of rich ground
that have been taken and made flesh
by them in that hidden place.

Funeral Piece

Life's mask
dropped off.
Death's is
your metaphor
now and
yours its
figure's face,
not to be
unmasked;
you go
too far
if it's
pulled away.

Imperishable

across
between
behind
below

are the imperishables

stored
as usual

fruits
by
access
to can

wise old man
had a cellar full

Bill As A Tree With One Live Branch

One limb of you
still lives enough
to branch into dreams
whose leaves leave,
and as far as it goes
all there is
in dreams is sleep
and dreams of you've
dropped gold aground.

Bill As Bell

not that you were
but if you had been--
say each of us
was and is--
a unit of sound;
the sound of you,
the you of you,
would--as it did--
resonate and carry:
a bell that
as it rings rings
its own and all
sounds' glory
overlaying silence
as all of us--
we and you--
did and do

Electric Shock

discovered
the secret of
your electricity
isn't either
yours or secret
nor yet electric
but of shock
enough
and

enough
and

enough

for direct
substantivesecret
claim

Your Poems

You saved
words chosen
to save you--

built of them
dwelt with them.

The words stand
and you lie
inviolable within.

Memorial

Not here--photographs,
paintings, sculpture:
not you;
speakers, readers, weepers,
flowers, and booklets--
none could conjure.
But
for you reading your poems,
even taped and replayed,
your ghost came
and filled the room
as your bass baritone
spoke imperative,
"...me, oh, look at me..."
and so we looked
and were trembled.

If Richard's Dream About Bill Were Mine

If sleep, in its universal language,
named what you gave me
it could be a comb,
a diamond comb, a 10 hardness
to comb through the dirt
and stone of this hard world,
one that will catch ablaze
when it touches the molten core.
Awake, no word says
what it is, has done.

His Reader

A man I knew
put the part of him
that was enchanted
into words so even
after he died when
they were read or spoken
or heard, he lived;
but this isn't all
I know of him
from that enthrallment.

The Sorcerer's Apprentice

My old master never said
what the magic was that
in presenting one thing
brought another,
but called it by its holy name
the lifetime of his practice.
Of what he taught me
that I can tell--
some mysteries must remain
silent and arcane
in bond of blood--
possibility comes through openness,
openness runs through fears,
and fear comes willy-nilly.
What you call it
is part of the name
you must speak
when you are apprenticed.

Kissing The Old Man

Whenever he materializes--
comes back, appears, puts on
human flesh, returns to earthly form--
however it's done, however I call it,
whatever it is or isn't, when that happens
I rush to him and sometimes take his hand,
as warm and solid as my own, or hug him hard,
feeling his body against mine undeniably
in the here and now--in the present--
seen and felt and here.

All this is prelude to the kiss,
that salute that I always offer
that he always accepts and returns.
This, the sign of our connectedness
that I long for, both to give and receive,
is as well the signal that he will go now,
this hello is also goodbye, the one
becoming the other as soon as it happens
and only in the tiny, immeasurable moment
of its contact, in the kiss of the kiss,
do we exchange what is otherwise impossible.

Guided Tour

My guide through the underworld
most often is an old man
who could command anything of me
but who saying nothing requires only
that I bow and lets me know
this needs doing because I find myself
bowing whenever he appears.
Containing his energy for him are
the shape and shade of a dead friend
whose face I kiss hello when I lift
my head after greeting that other.
From their benign junction I've
been taken to the world
where only spirit can go--
and I am back to tell that
there are great mysteries there,
not least of these that passage
and return had been arranged for me.

My Muse As Caesar

Under the hemlocks
in a straight back chair
Caesar sits surveying
the Celtic frontiers--
that is to say,
my heart--
over which island
nightly in its black sky
a mass of stars
resolves itself into
the Little Dipper
whose pivot adheres
in its constant place
and around it
all poems revolve.
It is as you command,
Caesar.

My Muse In The Guise Of Death And Vice Versa

My friends go up and down elevators
searching for poems I've misplaced
while I, looking in other rooms,
have found abed an old don,
a gracious gentleman.
Introduced, he kisses my hand
as I curtsey and I think
for now the lost poems
aren't as important as meeting
this ambassador of a foreign state
with whom I'm sure later
to be intimately acquainted.
Already I sense I know him well;
and then the poems turn up
and I leave his room for them.
"Come again," he whispers
in his old, velvet voice,
"Come again."

Two More For My Muse

I

My Muse Turns On Me

I went to my muse's house.
"What are you doing here?" he said.
"Go home to your husband."

II

How We Left It

After the hurt surprise,
the rejection, the warning
against mean, nasty behavior,
we settled in to a kind of conversation--
not about us--
concerning his other work.
He had drinks and cigarettes.
"Back at it?" I asked him.
"We wouldn't do this ordinarily."
He said nothing but offered them to me.
I guess we're on his terms,
we always were
whether I admitted it or not
and I didn't leave when I could have--
if I ever could.

imperfectives

Imperfective

Art doesn't have
to be perfect
because anything
might do it.

When just a single
word sings back
it's saying,
"Hear this"
as it vibrates.
"This is more than this."

Rhyme and rhythm
though they please us
are not what
we're listening for—
that is beyond pleasure
though the mouth
of its offer
kisses when it speaks
even what we are
afraid to hear
and we feel as if
the plates of the earth
rode up in us.

This is what has been
waiting for us.

Homestead

Your heart's fist-sized
grip and squeeze
has a farmer's job
but no twice a day here--
heart's husbandry's relentless,
draws to it incessant
circulations that are
incessantly pumped away,
cultivates the iambics
we speak and write,
gives constancy its name
for loves, deep intentions,
secret meanings, the very center
of this acreage upon which
we have been bred
and raised and made
the ready stock.

My Word On It

Tell them that the long blue vein
running down my writing arm
goes directly to the place
where blood can redeem us all.
Upon that circulation
you can say that I say that
more than the flow of words depends.

Lessons

My insatiable wants me
open to darkness;
everything--deadness,
envy, inertia--
must be learned. I ponder
what can be left out.

The Metaphor's Trick

Unasked for,
it showed me
what I'd be like without it,
revealing itself as
a kind of illusion
I was party to.
Glamourless, it
exposed us in our indigence,
sole and deficient.
Then it made me
reclaim what
it and I had been.

Rapt

You know and I know
when raptures as raptors
fly up through the dark,
through that tunnel in the dark,
and flash their underside
feathers, streaked and white,
they are displaying
to us and, their prey,
we see them
just before they hunt.

Vessels

Full as you imagine I am,
I am still empty enough to hold more.
We're containers meant to carry
back to each other
what we have brewed for ourselves.
Pour me full measure.
Yours is here.

Pilot

Under extraordinary circumstances
I pilot a tree,
flying horizontally
branches first at breathtaking speed,
to tell you.
I'm flying to tell you
that the circumstances are extraordinary,
that this tree
is more than it seems,
that anything you might name
could fly
given these conditions.

Pushover

Did I pull over
or was I pushed?
I don't care; I'm here--
supple and ready.
I almost wonder
when it happened,
but I'm busy
with the other thing.

Social Calendar

Poem and I require
only each other,
find the unit in
which we're contained
contains all we want.
Here is no schedule
nor appointments,
unsupervised words make
the calendar and our own purpose
designates the days
that we are meeting
with only ourselves.
We could call them holidays,
but this closed society
has done away with time
as it has all other markers
unrelated to our sorority.

The Hammock: From A Phrase By Thomas Mann

Gone
to sleep
in the life of the day
and dreamed
hammocked in day's life
tied at both ends
to everlasting dark
while netted and swaying
the shimmerous
knots of living
stretch tight.

Drink

I am hunting
with this full glass
all the thirsty spirits
in my soul.
Wine is blood
as blood is wine--
how we lap it up!
Then I hear
their voices
telling me the secrets
of their lives.
They want to talk
and tell me all,
and there are no surprises;
yet, heard the first time,
something old may
seem something new,
and because it's
the wine talking
and listening, too,
I write everything down.

love
in the second half of life

Love In The Second Half Of Life

I spoke too soon
when I said love
wasn't enough to keep me
here in the second half of life.
I spoke of mind and body's decline
as of a solstice–coming,
slow but surely coming–
and how I'd hate the long, cold dark of it.
So I would. But I see suddenly
that love is the only thing
to say to that; not
I won't or I can't or
how I hate the thought of it,
but I see love is the only thing:
that if I don't have it, nothing matters
and if I have it, nothing else matters.
I see I have begun now
to not care who loves me back.

What She Wept For

My friend cried on the phone;
her philandering liar had left her.
"After forty years," she kept saying.
"How could he after forty years?"
She thinks she's weeping for him,
their nice dinners and long walks,
but it's for the invisible she's crying--
the essential guts of time
which make a body of the years
we lie down with and which
hold it upright when we stand.

Bogey As My Dad

Don't think I haven't noticed
that those old movie stars
remind me of my father:
brushed-back hair, cigarette dangling,
glass of whiskey in hand.
There is an undeniable resemblance
in style and a congruity of time,
but it was what they did
that counted. They taught
me to believe in love,
to believe that there were men--
guys good and honest, or not,
tough or tender, drunk or sober--
but anyway, men who believed in love,
who would do anything
to have it and preserve it.
Of course, I wanted to believe--
God knows, I did and do--
and because when the student is ready
and the teacher appears,
when the learning takes place
it never needs to be learned again;
and a girl all her life loves like a father
the man who taught her that.

Kissing Time

When asked the time
my dad would say,
"Half-past kissin' time,
time to kiss again."
I don't know what went wrong:
the premise seems so sound.
It must have been
the times between,
in the unkissed
minutes and hours
when my father
became acquainted
with the concerns
that kept him out late
until kissing time
had come and gone and
our house went on
to standard time.

Instructional

Love and hate
are twin teaching tools
life employs to get us
to pay attention
to all the details
of its lessons.
If one method won't work,
the other usually does.
Remedial classes require
specialized skills;
life knows them all.

Long Division

My mind divides
to walk the afternoon
of its day, half here
watching itself
plan the evening;
when sun lights
in the branches,
as if luminous birds
came to roost
in these trees,
it loses track
of time.

Gordian Knot

Time is picking apart the knot
that life has made of me,
pulling loose single strands
and laying them out.
Kinked together in a tangle
for so long, my picaresques
permanently incline toward bosh
and the besom, the robust and ridiculous
alike bear an imprint of bliss
and time doesn't care about
the unmaking of what's
due to go under straight's blade.

Party Clothes

"Eternity is in love with the forms of time."   Joseph Campbell

Life is like that floral-patterned
see-through blouse I wore once
to a party where the light was dim.
It wasn't till I danced with someone
that he saw through it and stared.
Life, the teaser, dresses like that
and all the forms of time want to dance.
Then dancing, looking through
to naked shape, look further still:
seeing breasts--flesh's fruit--
see how, ripe, they contain their own decay,
how joy and sorrow come of the same thing,
are the same thing, only separated briefly
to be partners for this dance.

The Addition

My darling built an addition to me--
not the darling of my flesh, even he
can't make bricks of the mud and mortar me
up in a wider space, solid and high.
No, it's the other one that sponsors me
for unknown purposes who has lately
knocked out one old wall to encompass more.
From the new room, I have a bigger view;
I spend all of my free time here now.

Mazed

The answer
amazes me;
made intricate,
labyrinthine,
I repeat myself,
my disbelief,
and ask again.

RSVP

Rummaging through
the pockets of time
I found
that invitation I
answered yes to.
When I said,
"Yes, I'll come.
Let's go as far
as we can and
see where we end up,"
I didn't know
how long it would take
to go so short a way.

Reminder

A road is following me.
I look out the car window
and there--
traveling as I travel,
off to the side--
it goes under the trees,
sunglazed, then
out of sight over a hill.
I think time sends it
to tease me about eternity,
sends it as a picture
so I won't forget
it's not the turn-off
to the golden road
I'm looking for
but the way to be
that shock I feel
when I see it,
the recognition,
that moment
over a hill when the road
and I disappear.

Vehicular

Now neither driven nor driver
and not to be either again,
I will sit in the old seat sometimes,
sniff the old smells, try the old thoughts.
They don't go anywhere and neither do I.

The Old Thrill-Seekers

We tried it all--
drank beyond excitement,
smoked our atmosphere hazy,
we ate peyote, threw up,
and climbed trees
to be nearer the moon--.
Look what's become of us:
some fat, some drunk, some
respectable, a few all three.
What we used to seek
in our sleek, new bodies
had as little to do with
the ways we sought it
as numbers with infinity
or hours with the eternal.
The real thrill comes late,
then the moon comes down
through the trees to us,
and we must decide
how to embrace it.

Half Full

Cheerful people—
you know the type—
can't bear sorrow
as the sad can.
She breaks a wine glass in the sink:
"Thank God it wasn't on the floor."
She drops it on the floor:
"At least it wasn't full of wine."
It falls full:
"There's more in the bottle."
The bottle's empty:
"There's a store just down the road."

You see how it is:
bad can't be faced
so it's made into
something else.
This startle response
to life's surprises
is our innate defense
that changes nothing.
A glass is broken,
the floor needs cleaning up,
wine's spilled, and if
the store is closed
there'll be a long wait.
The trick is to learn
how to no longer
be taken by surprise,
to be astonished
all the time
at life indefensible.

Personal Shortcomings In A Great Man

You had to laugh
at the parsimony--
the downright cheapness--
that let half and half
curdle in coffee
before he'd buy new.
"Put a little soda in the carton,"
he'd say. "Use it up."
It was the same
with his frank and flawless vanity
which let him know
that his poems were high art
and that he was their chosen.
As for his and their lack of fame,
"A prophet goes without honor
in his own country" was his
assessment of that.
Where his greatness lay
was not in his gifts,
anyone might have gifts--
and faults, too, for that matter--
but in his transcendence of them.
He knew that they and he and all of us
didn't matter. But he said of this,
"It matters that it doesn't matter,"
and lived his life free.

Hemlocks

My trees out front
lean toward each other
at angles of intimacy
that draw me to them.
Beneath their
boughs' deep suspend
I stand intermediary
of what I would have
be mine and what is
empty space between them.

Used Book Store

I like to shop for books
where I don't know what
I might find. I let fate
or chance or both take a hand
in my education;
and those two have used books
as some men do dogs,
to track down the missing.
Time and again I've been found
closed up as if lost on some shelf
in a dark, narrow aisle--
unregarded, unimagined until
the volume and pages of me there
were opened and read
and so freed to partake
in the constant search
for more of the story.

The Bust-Up

Life is breaking up with me
and taking back all the presents
he gave that I thought
were a show of his love.
Ha, his love. He doesn't have to say
he's tired of me--I'm no fool.
He doesn't come around
like he used to when I and he
were new, were intimate and entwined
together in the most delicious adventures
anyone could ask for. He made me
feel that I was special--his darling,
his beloved--not his only, I knew that,
but close to him, always in his embrace.
Now, more and more often
I am alone while life is elsewhere
with others doing with them
what we used to do together.
I don't think I can live
without him. I don't want to.

Increased Forgetfulness As The Waning Moon

When I turned from this slowly begun
confusion of days and dates and numbers--
names for things forgotten, faces, others--
I saw the risen moon and there my mind,
both reflecting truly from their sources,
for in white moonlight there's pale hint of sun
as from blurred and blurring differences
mind shows, as of itself, how all is one.

ABOUT THE AUTHOR

Sherry Moore Kearns' writing has appeared in the following publications: *Transition, Blueline, Poetry New York, The Glens Falls Review, Sagetrieb, The Greenfield Review, North Country Review, The Body of This Life* (Talisman House, 2001) and *The Facts on File Companion to 20th-Century American Poetry* (Facts on File, Inc., 2005).

She is the author of the chapbooks *Sister* (Poetry New York, 1999) and *The Ginko at 57 Pearl St.* (James L. Weil, 2005). SUNY Adirondack published her essays *Conversations About Poetry* as part of their poetry and art series inspired by the William Bronk Collection.

A past recipient of a grant from New York State's Creative Artists Public Service (CAPS) program, Kearns also received the William Bronk Foundation prize for her memoir *Meeting Bill.*

Books by Dos Madres Press

Mary Margaret Alvarado - *Hey Folly* (2013)

John Anson - *Jose-Maria de Heredia's Les Trophées* (2013)

Jennifer Arin - *Ways We Hold* (2012)

Michael Autrey - *From The Genre Of Silence* (2008)

Paul Bray - *Things Past and Things to Come* (2006), *Terrible Woods* (2008)

Jon Curley - *New Shadows* (2009), *Angles of Incidents* (2012)

Sara Dailey - *Earlier Lives* (2012)

Richard Darabaner - *Plaint* (2012)

Deborah Diemont - *Wanderer* (2009), *Diverting Angels* (2012)

Joseph Donahue - *The Copper Scroll* (2007)

Annie Finch - *Home Birth* (2004)

Norman Finkelstein - *An Assembly* (2004), *Scribe* (2009)

Gerry Grubbs - *Still Life* (2005), *Girls in Bright Dresses Dancing* (2010)

Ruth D. Handel - *Tugboat Warrior* (2013)

Richard Hague - *Burst, Poems Quickly* (2004),
 During The Recent Extinctions (2012)

Pauletta Hansel - *First Person* (2007), *What I Did There* (2011)

Michael Heller - *A Look at the Door with the Hinges Off* (2006),
 Earth and Cave (2006)

Michael Henson - *The Tao of Longing & The Body Geographic* (2010)

R. Nemo Hill - *When Men Bow Down* (2012)

W. Nick Hill - *And We'd Understand Crows Laughing* (2012)

Eric Hoffman - *Life At Braintree* (2008), *The American Eye* (2011),
 By The Hours (2013)

James Hogan - *Rue St. Jacques* (2005)

Keith Holyoak - *My Minotaur* (2010), *Foreigner* (2012)

David M. Katz - *Claims of Home* (2011)

Burt Kimmelman - *There Are Words* (2007), *The Way We Live* (2011)

Pamela L. Laskin - *Plagiarist* (2012)

Richard Luftig - *Off The Map* (2006)

Austin MacRae - *The Organ Builder* (2012)

J. Morris - *The Musician, Approaching Sleep* (2006)

Rick Mullin - *Soutine* (2012), *Coelacanth* (2013)

Robert Murphy - *Not For You Alone* (2004), *Life in the Ordovician* (2007),
 From Behind The Blind (2013)

Pam O'Brien - *The Answer To Each Is The Same* (2012)

Peter O'Leary - *A Mystical Theology of the Limbic Fissure* (2005)

Bea Opengart - *In The Land* (2011)

David A. Petreman - *Candlelight in Quintero - bilingual edition* (2011)

Paul Pines - *Reflections in a Smoking Mirror* (2011), *New Orleans Variations & Paris Ouroboros* (2013)

David Schloss - *Behind the Eyes* (2005)

William Schickel - *What A Woman* (2007)

Lianne Spidel & Anne Loveland - *Pairings* (2012)

Murray Shugars - *Songs My Mother Never Taught Me* (2011), *Snakebit Kudzu* (2013)

Nathan Swartzendruber - *Opaque Projectionist* (2009)

Jean Syed - *Sonnets* (2009)

Madeline Tiger - *The Atheist's Prayer* (2010), *From the Viewing Stand* (2011)

James Tolan - *Red Walls* (2011)

Henry Weinfield - *The Tears of the Muses* (2005), *Without Mythologies* (2008), *A Wandering Aramaean* (2012)

Donald Wellman - *A North Atlantic Wall* (2010), *The Cranberry Island Series* (2012)

Anne Whitehouse - *The Refrain* (2012)

Martin Willetts Jr. - *Secrets No One Must Talk About* (2011)

Tyrone Williams - *Futures, Elections* (2004), *Adventures of Pi* (2011)

Kip Zegers - *The Poet of Schools* (2013)

www.dosmadres.com